FOREWORD

Every girl has a story, and so every girl needs a voice.

Through my past social justice work, I've learned in depth about girls' education and health issues through interviews, reports, research, conferences, and more. And through my advocacy work with various nonprofits I've realized this: the most powerful way to help is to hear from girls themselves.

64 Voices is a compilation of girls' stories across the world. Every story here is unique and personal to the author – the entries talk about a variety of sensitive topics, ranging from experiencing life as transgender women, dealing with physical disabilities, facing sexism at school, attending all-girls schools, battling severe mental health issues, and more. Regardless of the topic, each story is equally important and heartfelt.

These diverse stories have been collected from girls aged 11-28. In addition, these girls span 11 countries across the world and 8 states within the United States of America. Even though the girls are different physically, mentally, geographically, financially, and socially, there are common themes in their experiences, which is a notable pattern to encounter.

The intention of my book, which is one of the initiatives of my larger nonprofit Uplifting-Her, is to create a safe space for girls and young women to discuss anything that may be on their minds, connect and unite with others, and provide advice. Together, if we listen to stories from other young women, we can help each other and make a difference. And if we share our own stories, we can help ourselves, which is just as important.

I hope that all the girls who have contributed to this book know how deeply thankful I am for having the courage to share their voices. By reading the other 63 stories included, I hope that each girl can realize that although their life experiences are their own, they are not alone. As mentioned, so many of their stories overlap and discuss similar life occurrences despite being written through individual lenses.

Thank you so much. I hope that you are as moved and touched as I have been by each girl's voice, story, and experience. Enjoy the book!

Love,
Anya

LIST OF CONTRIBUTORS

These stories have been contributed by girls and young women from 11 countries around the world. Three of the 64 stories are being published based on translation of their stories shared in Hindi (audio) to English. In certain instances, our contributors have chosen a pseudonym or indicated that they want to be anonymous. An asterisk (*) next to a name indicates that the contributor chose to use a pseudonym.

Story Number 1: **Fatima**	age: 14 years	Karachi, Pakistan
Story Number 2: **DB***	age: 21 years	New York, USA
Story Number 3: **Survi**	age: 22 years	Bihar, India
Story Number 4: **BA***	age: 18 years	UK
Story Number 5: **Ukyung**	age: 20 years	Busan, South Korea
Story Number 6: **SG***	age: 17 years	New York, USA
Story Number 7: **Nupur**	age: 23 years	Washington DC, USA
Story Number 8: **Isha**	age: 16 years	New York, USA
Story Number 9: **Elena**	age: 20 years	Illinois, USA
Story Number 10: **Muskaan**	age: 20 years	Michigan USA
Story Number 11: **Sara**	age: 11 years	Pennsylvania, USA
Story Number 12: **Kira***	age: 15 years	New Jersey, USA
Story Number 13: **Aliya**	age: 19 years	BC, Canada
Story Number 14: **Grishmaa A***	age: 16 years	Maharashtra, India
Story Number 15: **Cass***	age: 17 years	New York, USA

Story Number 16: **JD***   age: 17 years   New York, USA

Story Number 17: **Smiti**   age: 22 years   Haryana, India

Story Number 18: **Naisha**   age: 18 years   Maharashtra, India

Story Number 19: **Alia**   age: 19 years   New York, USA

Story Number 20: **Sansriti**   age: 28 years   USA

Story Number 21: **Ava**   age: 16 years   New York, USA

Story Number 22: **Cate**   age: 16 years   New York, USA

Story Number 23: **Pigeon***   age: 18 years   New York, USA

Story Number 24: **Mika***   age: 16 years   Pennsylvania USA

Story Number 25: **Sophia**   age: 16 years   New York, USA

Story Number 26: **Caelyn**   age: 17 years   New York, USA

Story Number 27: **Rani**   age: 18 years   New Jersey, USA

Story Number 28: **Lauren**   age: 16 years   New Jersey, USA

Story Number 29: **Judy**   age: 17 years   New Jersey, USA

Story Number 30: **Michelle**   age: 19 years   Washinton DC, USA

Story Number 31: **Ilyssa**   age: 19 years   Massachusetts, USA

Story Number 32: **Sophia**   age: 18 years   New York, USA

Story Number 33: **Ari**   age: 19 years   New York, USA

Story Number 34: **Anonymous-1*** age: 16 years   New York, USA

Story Number 35: **Anya**   age: 18 years   New York, USA

Story Number 36: **Eileen**   age: 16 years   New York, USA

Story Number 37: **Amelia***	age: 13 years	Maharashtra, India
Story Number 38: **Bhumi**	age: 20 years	Chattisgarh, India
Story Number 39: **Siddhi "Sakshi"**	age: 22 years	Chattisgarh, India
Story Number 40: **Saburi**	age: 26 years	Chattisgarh, India
Story Number 41: **Hannah**	age: 18 years	New York, USA
Story Number 42: **N.P.***	age: 14 years	Maharashtra, India
Story Number 43: **Kate***	age: 14 years	California, USA
Story Number 44: **Israt**	age: 16 years	Barishal District, Bangladesh
Story Number 45: **Kayla**	age: 16 years	Pennsylvania, USA
Story Number 46: **Tanya**	age: 12 years	New York, USA
Story Number 47: **A.S.***	age: 19 years	New York, USA
Story Number 48: **Anonymous-2***	age: undisclosed	Barishal District, Bangladesh
Story Number 49: **Anonymous-3***	age: undisclosed	Barishal District, Bangladesh
Story Number 50: **Anonymous-4***	age: undisclosed	Barishal District, Bangladesh
Story Number 51: **Sharaban**	age: undisclosed	Barishal District, Bangladesh
Story Number 52: **Anonymous-5***	age: undisclosed	Barishal District, Bangladesh
Story Number 53: **Afrin**	age: undisclosed	Barishal District, Bangladesh
Story Number 54: **Sapto**	age: undisclosed	Barishal District, Bangladesh
Story Number 55: **Anonymous-6***	age: undisclosed	Barishal District, Bangladesh
Story Number 56: **Anan**	age: undisclosed	Barishal District, Bangladesh
Story Number 57: **Ayesha**	age: undisclosed	Barishal District, Bangladesh

Story Number 58: **Ansha**	age: undisclosed	Barishal District, Bangladesh
Story Number 59: **Rabia**	age: undisclosed	Barishal District, Bangladesh
Story Number 60: **Sarina**	age: 16 years	New York, NY
Story Number 61: **Pigeon-2***	age: 19 years	Guadalajara, Jalisco, Mexico
Story Number 62: **Momo***	age: 20 years	Uganda
Story Number 63: **Ljubica**	age: 26 years	Pichincha, Quito, Ecuador
Story Number 64: **Sage Voyageur***	age: 24 years	Bujumbura, Burundi

Note:
All stories contributed in English have been published reflecting grammar and spelling specific to the contributors' geographic regions. No alterations have been made to conform to U.S. grammar or spelling conventions.

STORY NUMBER 1

FATIMA
age: 14 years
Karachi, Pakistan

I live in Karachi, Pakistan where girls education is not prioritized as much as boys education. Everyday schools are opening not with purpose of providing quality education but as a form of business. Handsome amounts of funds are taken by the locals or the government in the name of promoting girls education but nothing as such is done. No concrete action is taken for the girls. Many girls are forcefully married of after the age of 14. These practices need to be stopped for the country's civilisation and prosperity; as well as for the better welfare of the female population in the country.

◆ ◆ ◆

STORY NUMBER 2

DB*
age: 21 years
New York, USA

As a college student, one of the hardest things to identify and deal with is anxiety and stress. As someone who was used to not feeling stressed due to academics, I never thought I'd be someone who would experience stress or anxiety. And so, when due to social issues/dynamics with friends beyond my control, I started to feel anxiety due to uncertainty and stress in my social relationships, it was hard for me to identify it and identify the issues I was dealing with until those relationships eventually burnt out and I realized I had anxiety. Once I identified it, I was better able to manage and understand it with the support of my friends.

◆ ◆ ◆

STORY NUMBER 3

SURVI
age: 22 years
Bihar, India

My name is Survi and I'm from Bihar, India. I'm currently pursuing graduation in political science from Banaras Hindu University Varanasi. Since childhood I have been a person who use to be a support system for everybody. I believe in social service, I feel as if life is like a game and at the end what matters is how well we played this game, how much love we had spread in this world and how much love we got from this world. I'm a self motivated person, who had seen a lot of circumstances of life, many ups abd down which are the part of life. Officially I started my social work since 2019. I had work with different organisation like youth against injustice Foundation, Youwe, Vrikshit Foundation, Muskurahat Foundation etc. Since this journey I meant a lot of new people who are much more devoted towards the social work and I learned a lot from them. My life will always be ready for the social service.

◆ ◆ ◆

STORY NUMBER 4

BA*
age: 18 years
London, UK

Going to an all-girls school, I have been privileged to be in an environment where female education is not only so encouraged, but also given incredible resources. In my school, we really pride girls on independence and making their way in male-dominated spaces.

◆ ◆ ◆

STORY NUMBER 5

UKYUNG
age: 20 years
Busan, South Korea

I was lucky enough to have access to educational opportunities from a young age. If I wanted to learn something, my parents did not deny me. This is not to say that these environments were perfect–they weren't always friendly towards girls taking up space, which motivated me to create Malala Fund's first high school chapter at school–but they gave me more than enough: spaces that were safe to learn and grow in. Not many girls can say the same, especially not in less privileged parts of the world. For them, a shot at education is likely to come at a personal cost to their own health and happiness, due to the oppressive cultures and circumstances they are governed by. They may never experience the liberation that an education can give them in life, and my wish is to see the world changed in a way that they can. In order for this to happen, I believe we must bring more women's voices and faces to the forefront of all fields, especially the media. The impact of images is striking and far-reaching. Seeing a girl in your class become elected to a position of authority within the community is powerful. Seeing a female artist, caregiver, business owner and many more become spotlighted in newspapers and magazines is powerful. Such powerful sights set a vision, and that vision calls for more; not only for girls to want and strive for more, but for the community around them to think that girls deserve more. And such thoughts, once conceived, are bound to come true. In her essay "Women, Self-Possession and Sport", feminist and athlete Catherine Mackinnon posits the following; because female incapability and inferiority is thought (by men and women alike, but more so by men), it is embodied by women and becomes reality. We must utilize the same pipeline of thought to reality, but with thoughts of female power, potential, and proficiency, by populating the space of collective human thought with these notions.

◆ ◆ ◆

STORY NUMBER 6

SG*
age: 17 years
New York, USA

As a girl going into the physics major at my school, I was nervous. The year before me only had two girls in the entire major. I have been in math classes where there were few other girls but this was never the case in my core curriculum. The underestimation women receive in specifically STEM fields can make learning tiresome and I feared the constant need to prove myself. I was, though, lucky enough to walk into my first physics class and find that almost half of the students were girls! Not letting fear of sticking out stop me from following my interests allowed me to make such great connections, along with a stronger knowledge of physics and astronomy. To anyone who is nervous about entering a new environment without guarantee of peers like you, remember my positive experience and take the leap!

◆ ◆ ◆

STORY NUMBER 7

NUPUR
age: 23 years
Washington DC, USA

When I was in middle school, my mother had a brain tumor that caused her to black out often, but because of the frequent emesis that came with it, no doctors listened to her complaints of headaches and suggested that she stop eating such "spicy indian food" and opt for healthier options instead. After several ER visits and continued blackouts, one doctor out of the several who treated my mom finally decided to try a brain MRI and found a tumor the size of a golf ball at the base of her skull. It would've killed her had it not been removed in time and burst instead. Since then, my mother has gotten better but my faith in the American healthcare system and doctors is irrecoverably broken which is why I have dedicated myself to a career in patient advocacy and public health. No one should be cast aside or neglected the way my mother was just because an overworked health professional is unable to make the right call or listen to their patients; and I am working to better educate myself to prevent similar things from happening to people who aren't as fortunate as my mother because proper healthcare is a human right.

◆ ◆ ◆

STORY NUMBER 8

ISHA
age: 16 years
New York, USA

I have IBS and it interferes with life when I have a flare up. Not easy to deal with during the school year.

◆ ◆ ◆

STORY NUMBER 9

ELENA
age: 20 years
Illinois, USA

I had a difficult time my freshman year of college, adjusting to living in a new place, being around new people, and struggling with classes all at the same time. I think that if I was only experiencing one of the three things above I would have faced less mental health issues, but since I was really struggling to be motivated in school, being in an unfamiliar environment definitely escalated my issues. I found it hard to open up to my new friends about how I was feeling since I felt like they were having a good college experience and I didn't want to burden them with my problems. Looking back, I'm so glad I managed to make it through that year and go back to college for my sophomore year because things got significantly better my second year. I think knowing that I had made it through such a hard time, coming back to school already familiar with my environment and being much closer to my friends, made my college experience way better. Even now when I'm going through rough patches in school I think about how much better things are now than they were 2 years ago and it helps me have a more positive outlook on my life.

◆ ◆ ◆

STORY NUMBER 10

MUSKAAN
age: 20 years
Michigan, USA

Middle school wasn't easy for me. Not because of classes, but because the people at school suddenly knew how to use their words, and they had opted to use them against me. It was in middle school that a boy made fun of me for having a moustache, it was in middle school that my entire class seemed to turn against me because I was good at studies, it was in middle school that a girl told me I was a ***** whose face resembled that of a pig, and that I only had friends because they wanted to leach off of my academic success. I feel we sometimes dismiss the struggles of children, as though they couldn't possibly have experienced anything truly relevant in the time they've been alive. But middle school wasn't easy, and it left scars on me that I still continuously discover and have to work to heal at age 20.

◆ ◆ ◆

STORY NUMBER 11

SARA
age: 11 years
Pennsylvania, USA

Being an Indian-American kid is awesome! My parents came from India to chase their dreams, and they're totally rocking it! They're always working on exciting projects and it makes me want to dream big and make my own mark on the world too. School can be tricky sometimes, but I've learned that it's okay to face challenges. I enjoy discovering new things and figuring out what I excel at. The best part is getting to learn about my Indian heritage while experiencing all the amazing opportunities America has to offer. It feels like I have two huge backpacks filled with adventures! This gives me the confidence to aim high, no matter what. Even though I'm young, I'm eager to make a positive impact. I want to help people feel happy and confident. My parents believe I can achieve anything I set my mind to, and I believe them too! I can't wait to see what exciting adventures await me and how I can use my skills to contribute to making the world a better place.

◆ ◆ ◆

STORY NUMBER 12

KIRA*
age: 15 years
New Jersey, USA

I've always been interested in academics and in school I try to do my best work so I feel confident in my learning. When it comes to group projects in school, I've never been the strongest advocate. It's not that I dislike community or working with other people, but I don't enjoy having to delegate certain tasks to people or working with people who I know won't contribute to everyone else. There was one time where I was doing a biology project and I was paired with 3 other guys. We just had to make a slideshow explaining one phenomena we learned in the year in detail. When it came to actually working with them though, I felt like I couldn't express my ideas or provide a clear plan of how we should split up the work. When I tried to say how we should each take a section of the slideshow, I ended having to take on majority of the work, like finding almost all the information and creating the slides. They became unresponsive to my emails and other questions, even when we met in class. I told my teacher but she didn't take any action, so I ended up completing the presentation mostly by myself. Later, I heard them talking to one another about how they heard I had told my teacher and they were complaining that I hadn't even done that much work. I was jut being whiny. When we got back our grade, which was good, they ended up taking a lot of the credit for what I had done. It's frustrating to constantly be ignored by the people around you when you know that you put in so much effort and you don't get the recognition you deserve. My teacher didn't even seem to care.

◆ ◆ ◆

STORY NUMBER 13

ALIYA
age: 19 years
British Columbia, Canada

As a disabled woman of colour, I have spent my entire life being disregarded by health care. Over and over I described excruciating physical pain I was told I am dramatic, weak, or it must be my period. And my mental illness is used as the punchline of jokes to insinuate we are crazy or unstable. I have come to learn to trust my own mind and body. Until the day our health is taken as seriously as privilege groups, we will continue to suffer and die - but we will not go quietly.

◆ ◆ ◆

STORY NUMBER 14

GRISHMAA A*
age: 16 years
Maharashtra, India

Ever since childhood, I've always faced issues with fine motor actions, and frankly, I still do. However, my parents hoped they would go away with time assuming they were 'clumsy kid' things. It wasn't that they didn't try to help, but rather they always suggested activities that'd help me with my motor skills (my mother, being an educational psychology expert, was pretty informed about those). Still, I experienced many delayed milestones, i.e., I learned many little things way later than the ideal age (E.g, wearing a shirt at 8, doing my hair at 7, and brushing my teeth around the same age, I still can't tie a shoelace, etc). Although my parents always supported me and encouraged me to try & learn, my peers in primary school weren't so kind. A few incidents still sting like bruises. For example, when I was in 3rd grade, I had to tie my answer sheet to the supplementary sheet with a thread for the first time, and I was fumbling a little more than others. The supervisor said in a mocking tone to her colleague, "Oh, what a stupid child! Can't even turn a page properly and they say she's excelled in competitive exams! How's that even possible?" I still wonder how someone who says such things in front of a child could become a primary school teacher in the first place. It still feels like an ointment when someone kindly lends a hand to help me tie threads & laces. Furthermore, I also had a diurnal enuresis issue until almost this year. With growing age, I learned to hide away these motor impairments to save myself from embarrassment and humiliation which was way tougher than hiding my cognitive quirks. I had always been a huge introvert too, and I've had many traits that I later found out to be autism & ADHD symptoms. I developed a toxic coping mechanism to hide things happening in school from my parents, even got bullied by some seniors and no one knew. Middle school and high school were a huge relief. By then I'd learned to choose the right sort of people, had been educated about mental health and neurodiverse community, had started researching my symptoms, and tried to convince my parents to seek a diagnosis. Yet, bottling up the toxic memories from primary school led to mental health and eating disorders in high school. Many people I know would disagree with my next statement as I always get pretty good grades, though it's definitely true that I've never been able to take my scores up to my potential. This was thanks to me having to deal with anxiety as well as my resurfacing depression, hyperactivity, undiagnosed neurodevelopmental disorder, and an ED (though I must be utterly grateful to my friends and classmates in high school for always trying their best to never make me feel embarrassed of my conditions). Yet, I can surely claim one thing: the journey before passing out of high school eased many things for me, and moving out this year has now given me a renewed sense of hope to navigate a way back to finding my whole identity again. I'm certain that I've eventually reached a pedestal where I can avoid letting my cognitive struggles get in the way of my academic progress! I hope this is going to be an insightful journey ahead as well.

◆ ◆ ◆

STORY NUMBER 15

CASS*
age: 17 years
New York, USA

MENTAL HEALTH: I've struggled with eating disorders for what feels like forever. I can't remember a time where I haven't been obsessing over calories. Because I've struggled for so long it's become normal for me even though it's not normal. While my struggle never became "dangerous" because my health wasn't at risk, what I was doing wasn't healthy. Because I went from being kind of heavy to slimmer, I was praised for what I did even though it wasn't healthy. I think it is so important to talk about these issues especially as girls because a lot of eating disorders have been so normalized and it is really harmful for impressionable girls. I have always wanted to reach out to girls that share my experience because I think it is important that they can feel heard. I think that diet culture is something that is very prevalent everywhere and it can be difficult to recognize when there is truly a problem. I also think that eating disorders look very different for so many people that sometimes it can be difficult for girls to acknowledge that they might have one because it is not like someone else's. In school we have had discussions in health class with what eating disorders look like and I think that the approach is helpful. I think that projects such as these are so important because they really do give a light to people's voices who can speak for those who can't.

◆ ◆ ◆

STORY NUMBER 16

J.D*
age: 17 years
New York, USA

My experience as a female has been greatly shaped by the women of the Black Panther Party. In an organization that fought to empower African Americans, female members were subject to gender-discrimination by their male colleagues; as a consequence, the women's stories were erased from history. Nonetheless, these women stayed resolute and determined; they refused to let the men continue to suppress them to lesser roles. Consequently, the women overcame their challenges. Staying silent may often appear as the only viable option. Yet, we can reflect upon the women pioneers whose defiance led them to victory. These women remind us that, as women, we must do whatever we can in order to make our voices heard.

◆ ◆ ◆

STORY NUMBER 17

SMITI
age: 22 years
Haryana, India

I had a really fulfilling college experience overall, but found some parts to be challenging emotionally. Being in a high-achieving environment, I pushed myself beyond my limits. I got to a point where I wasn't able to tap as easily into the curiosity and critical thinking within myself, and frequently felt anxious. My gap year really helped me heal. I got some time off to work on projects that truly interested me, at my own pace. I also got time at home, in India, to connect with my family, travel, and re-ground. I underwent a thyroid surgery last year that took me out of college for a month. I was extremely grateful to have friends around that made it a priority to understand the specifics of my health and check in about what I could and couldn't participate in.

◆ ◆ ◆

STORY NUMBER 18

NAISHA
age: 18 years
Maharashtra, India

As a woman in STEM the gender disparity, that continues to exist today, has always been apparent. Most of my classes have always been dominated by men, while the females were usually quiet and somewhat ignored. Females continue facing subtle biases and occasional skepticism from peers and professors in the academic space, despite being equal in intellect.

◆ ◆ ◆

STORY NUMBER 19

ALIA
age: 19 years
New York, USA

I went to a pretty competitive high school which sometimes fostered a negative environment in which it was easy for mental health to be overlooked. This made a lot of us support and lean on our friends a lot more.

◆ ◆ ◆

STORY NUMBER 20

SANSRITI
age: 28 years
USA

Education has always been the thing I value most. I have always loved reading as a window into other experiences, as well as a mirror that can reflect my own experiences back at me and help me better make sense of them. Further, I truly believe that as a young, queer woman of color who is now an English teacher for high school students, representation in literature and empathy-building through diverse texts is something I am deeply passionate about.

◆ ◆ ◆

STORY NUMBER 21

AVA
age: 16 years
New York, USA

My own womanhood is something that I consider often, especially considering I am still somewhat of a girl. There's good and bad parts of that. Reflecting on feminism, though, the experiences of my grandmother differ from mine in half a million ways. Specifically, I want to say this: the feminism of my grandmother's generation was loud in order to combat loud hatred. However, I find my own adolescent battles mainly take place within myself. They are quietly fought. This isn't to say that my life won't become more complicated and extreme as I embark into the working world and find myself in claustrophobic rooms full of men. But the real misogyny I work to offset the most in my day-to-day life is internalized. For instance, I am always thinking about other people's reactions to me, even when they don't matter that much. I recognize this need to conform and people-please everywhere in women. I saw a video compilation of all of Nikki Haley's self-contradictions yesterday (more than a few) and I thought to myself 'she's just saying what she thinks they want to hear!' I don't agree with most of Nikki Haley's political views, but that desire to ingratiate is embarrassingly familiar to me. I kind of understood it. On the topic of other people's reactions to who I am, I know my growing body scares my family members sometimes, because the little baby they knew now has hips and breasts about the same width and size as their wife. And she wears bikinis. I've simultaneously become ashamed and proud of what I look like, when I'm trying and when I'm not. My body frustrates me often because I feel as though it's not something most men have to consider about themselves nearly as much as I do. My body is a political statement, no matter what I do with it. I ask myself cringey questions trying to figure out how I should dress and look: Is it feminist to show some tit? Am I REALLY doing it for myself? Is it okay if I'm not? I can't say it's not ridiculously confusing. In these situations I don't know what really can be considered feminist. I don't really think this struggle is new, but I guess my statement certainly highlights this conundrum and its permanence. Sometimes I wonder about how I would be if I wasn't a woman. I kind of see it reflected in my brother. He actively avoids apologizing, I apologize to inanimate objects for bumping into them. To put things bluntly, he takes up space without concern. I don't wish I wasn't a girl, but I am a world class ponderer. I ask myself: In a different skin, would I be healed from my affliction of eternal irrelevance? And I decide: If I were not contained in this body, I would not worry nearly as much about being loved. I would be happy to be feared. I know that my tangled mind would be worth much more. I knew that even at 7 years old. The unfortunate defense mechanisms we build out of self hatred from the youngest ages fascinate me, being someone who has definitely engaged in such a performance. Some girls run away as fast as they can from their own femininity to earn acceptance of a male audience. Others find out they get the same twisted acceptance by sexualizing themselves. It then becomes addictive, appealing to this council of men and boys who have the ability to decide whether they can treat you as a person or not. You spend years of your life trying to convince them of your valuable qualities. When I was much younger, if anyone asked me, my favorite color was blue. Not to say girls don't like the color blue, but my favorite colors were actually pink and purple, I just thought that's what all the other girls would say and I had decided I was going to set myself apart from them. Blue was my 3rd favorite. I played sports and when I wore dresses (of my own accord), I would announce to everyone that my mom made me wear it. I called myself weird and became obsessed with aliens and making ugly faces in pictures, partially a misguided attempt to escape this gender role I believed I was too gross to fit. This escape didn't work; I found myself just as unwanted as before. But it's not lost on me the actual thought process of such a phase: I thought defying all things feminine made me different and more interesting. Perhaps better. I wanted to be smart and strong, which I didn't think you could do if you were a girl, no matter how many glittery pink girl power t-shirts from Justice™ my parents and I bought. My feminist ideas have since evolved of course, and now since I work in an elementary school after school on Mondays, sometimes I recognize these traits in other little girls. I try to steer them on the right path, but unfortunately I've found that this conclusion, this self-acceptance of your own girlhood, is something a girl needs to reckon with on her own in order to eventually resent it less. I wish there was more I could be doing for feminism, I truly do. But instead I find myself writing whiny think pieces about how I hate feeling so weak in the eyes of others. How I could maybe one day be strong and command respect. About one day finally feeling comfort in who I am. And maybe that's my own feminism? For myself? And now, in this year 2024, as I talk about activism and myself, I also need to say that it's no longer just about being a man or a woman anymore. I don't think it ever was. It's about so much more - intersectionality, allyship, offering your support to people who want it. Striving for equality for everyone we know, even if that means it's not always about you. I have a lot to be thankful for, but the 'unfinishedness' of it all often strikes me. I can obviously speak for myself, but I don't know how to speak for my generation. Maybe I can only say my feminism/activism is an internal battle because I'm still in high school and my world is small. But overall, I think the older generations fought all kinds of these exhausting physical battles so I wouldn't have to. Not to say that my grandmother did not face internalized misogyny, but to underline the point that people just flat out told her she shouldn't do things because she was a woman. We diverge paths here because people don't often just say no to me and calmly explain that it's because I'm a woman, even if it is. They dance around their real issue with me, and the degradation is so subtle I'm left to feel embarrassed and confused with myself. While what I've just written outlines years more of painstaking work to be done, I'm eternally grateful for the initial feminist waves. When I remember this beautiful change we've experienced over time and the change that is yet to come, I try to love myself just a little bit more, despite everything I've said here. I try to stay motivated to live the life my grandmother made more attainable for me. My education is a gift, but I wish it could teach me and other people to love myself because I'm a woman, not in spite of it.

◆ ◆ ◆

STORY NUMBER 22

CATE
age: 16 years
New York, USA

As someone who used to go to a co-ed school and now goes to a historically single sex school, I have noticed a few differences. I think that the the girls who participate a lot in class at my current school would probably do the same if they went to coed schools, as that's how it was when I went to a coed school. I think that the girls who participate on occasion at my current school wouldn't participate at all if they went to a coed school, however, because they are encouraged to participate by the fact that there aren't a ton of people raising their hands. Of course, part of this is that the class size is smaller at my current school, but I also think that boys participate in class more often then girls do, so this lack of participation in a predominantly female environment encourages girls who wouldn't usually participate to do so. The biggest difference is sex education. At the co-ed school I went to we did sex education all together and the boys would always laugh all the time, but the girls would usually be quiet. It almost felt like the boys were laughing at a joke that we weren't in on. At my current school, we all giggle from time to time but it feels more like we are uncomfortable together. All in all, I don't think that going to a predominantly female school is necessarily better, it's just different.

◆ ◆ ◆

STORY NUMBER 23

PIGEON*
age: 18 years
New York, USA

I've always loved engineering and STEM in general. In high school, I took a particularly challenging Physics course. I was lucky enough to have other girls in my class, as we were able to support each other. We regularly studied together and collaborated on problem sets, and we always made sure every question and idea was heard.

◆ ◆ ◆

STORY NUMBER 24

MIKA*
age: 16 years
Pennsylvania, USA

Academics have taken a toll on my mental health, often generating stress and anxiety. It has caused me to take mental health more seriously and focus more on my well being. It's important to remember that we are not alone and there are many other people dealing with the same issues. You should always communicate with your family and friends, relaying your thoughts and feelings, instead of keeping them bottled up. For those who are battling mental health issues, remember that help is always available!

◆ ◆ ◆

STORY NUMBER 25

SOPHIA
age: 16 years
New York, USA

In seventh grade, I was in my humanities class talking to my teacher about an assignment, and a boy came up to the teacher and tried to interrupt me while I was speaking to her. When I stopped him and politely asked if I could finish speaking, he called me a h*e and ran out of the classroom.

◆ ◆ ◆

STORY NUMBER 26

CAELYN
age: 17 years
New York, USA

I grew up overweight as a multicultural girl. As a result, I had a lot of animosity toward my body and my weight that I never properly solved until I really worked on self love. A lot of times, women- especially women of color- are screwed over in the medicine industry. Our health is reduced to a weight problem without acknowledging our ethnicity, cultural diet, and doctors gender bias. Learning about my cultural identity as well as how weight presents on a woman, really improved my self-esteem and understanding. Our pain is often not taken seriously in the medicine world. For example, I went to the doctor- a male- for pain in my wrist, and it was written off as pain that would simply go away. Still I scheduled an MRI (which I haven't done yet) and my wrist pain has continued for months. As a result, I am currently wearing a brace until I can get the MRI and understand what is truly wrong. Education on the subject of health is essential for women as we are living in a society that isn't made for us. Our bodies don't work on a 24 hour cycle which mens do. We have to work on a hormone cycle that goes against our body and function day-to-day. Learning about my body and my health as well as my ethnicity as a mixed woman opened my eyes; and made me begin to understand how to help my own body.

◆ ◆ ◆

STORY NUMBER 27

RANI
age: 18 years
New Jersey, USA

I think that fact that I have a female pediatrician has made my experience with physical health really great. My doctor is very well versed in women health issues and has given great advice in regards to birth control, period health, and other facets a male doctor may not be able to understand.

◆ ◆ ◆

STORY NUMBER 28

LAUREN
age: 16 years
New Jersey, USA

Growing up, I have always been shy and reserved. In elementary school I often had many ideas in my head but refrained from participating in class. I was like by my teachers because I was quiet and respectful. In groups, I was often paired with the louder boys, being an "easier" child. Additionally, there was a big ratio of girls to boys in my grade, with there being few girls. My parents and I felt that I was often looked past in school and had a lot of distractions. I decided, with the advice of my parents, to go to an all girls school for middle and high school. I feel I have finally come out of my shell and been able to find my voice at my school. My school's emphasis on the importance of girls' education is empowering and inspiring. Today, I am outgoing, curious and have a love for learning!

◆ ◆ ◆

STORY NUMBER 29

JUDY
age: 17 years
New York, USA

In my culture, there isn't blatant discrimination against women as there was in the past due to the changing times. However, there has remained a discrepancy in female representation and male representation in specific professions, such as in the medical or law fields. In Korean culture, mainly men take on these professions, and women are discouraged from pursuing higher education such as a master's or a pHD because these educations are male-dominated. I recently did a program from Perry Initiative, which empowers women and encourages them to go into medicine, engineering, or orthopedic surgery. This experience made me realize that women are still struggling with being adequately represented in certain fields.

◆ ◆ ◆

STORY NUMBER 30

MICHELLE
age: 19 years
Washington DC, USA

As a female student, I have never felt uncomfortable or silenced in any of my academic environments. As I pursue business and enter a more male-dominated field, I hope to remember and look back at what has helped me stay focused and grounded during my academic career.

◆ ◆ ◆

STORY NUMBER 31

ILYSSA
age: 19 years
Massachusetts, USA

I went to an all girls high school and have always felt it's important to advocate for women in the workplace, in underrepresented fields(STEM), and in positions of power.

◆ ◆ ◆

STORY NUMBER 32

SOPHIA
age: 18 years
New York, USA

When I was growing up, all I wanted to do was do the same activities as my older brother. Christo started playing baseball when he was four, so I started playing baseball when I was four. Christo went to the Baseball Center on 74th Street on Wednesday nights to work on his hitting, so I started going too. I loved playing little league baseball every weekend, and on my baseball team and at school, it didn't seem to matter that I was a girl. I still got MVP awards after games, I started at first base every weekend, and I loved playing pickup wiffle ball in the basement at school during recess with the boys, many of whom were some of my best friends at the time. But during third or fourth grade, things started to change. My brother and the other boys at school started joining travel baseball clubs, which got to travel to tournaments in Connecticut and Maryland. But most travel clubs didn't allow girls to join. In little league, the number of other girls diminished until I was the only girl on my team and almost never saw girls on the other teams. More importantly, the boys at school started excluding me from baseball during recess, telling me that I wasn't good enough to keep up with them. It didn't matter that we were all the same height or that I could hit the ball just as far as them—the older we got, the more separated the boys became from the girls, and I gradually lost a lot of my male friends. In middle school, I joined softball instead of baseball, and even though I enjoyed playing with just girls, this gap seemed to become even more insurmountable. These days, my brother and I are still extremely close and love all of the same things. Even though he's in college, we still call a few times a month to talk about baseball or fun facts about trains or how to fix the latest bug in my Python code. But the difference between the things I couldn't do that Christo could during our childhood still sticks out to me. Even though it was just baseball, the overall increase of gender-exclusive social spaces and activities negatively impacted my educational experience as a girl.

◆ ◆ ◆

STORY NUMBER 33

ARI
age: 19 years
New York, USA

Growing up, I had always played soccer and it was a large part of my life. I was on a travel team and practices and games consumed a large part of my life. For middle school, my family moved to Japan and I quickly learned that the opportunities for girls to play soccer were much smaller. In the fall of 6th grade, I joined the co-ed soccer team, but was only one of two girls on the team. I ended up playing on the co-ed team for one year and the girls team in the spring for two years, but eventually I dropped soccer because it was draining and not fair for me to play against teams that were all boys and much bigger than me. Eventually I switched to playing volleyball, which I grew to love, but I wish there were more opportunities for girls to thrive and play soccer there.

◆ ◆ ◆

STORY NUMBER 34

ANONYMOUS-1*
age: 16 years
New York, USA

It can be really difficult to be one of the only women in certain classes because a lot of men do not understand what that does to your confidence or how you conduct yourself in class. While studies have shown that women do better at test taking when they are surrounded by other women, people still don't take this lack of representation as an issue. Truthfully, it has turned me off of going into STEM fields and made me feel like the only thing I am good at is the humanities because I am so much more comfortable in the latter.

◆ ◆ ◆

STORY NUMBER 35

ANYA
age: 18 years
New York, USA

I have been lucky so far in my life and haven't experienced lots of discrimination because of my sex. I am a musician, and am going into percussion as a career. I have had many supportive teachers who don't view me as less than a man…though I have realized recently that almost all of my music teachers have been men. I never truly thought about this or the impact it has made on me until my percussion teacher's own teacher from years ago assumed I couldn't play fff on timpani because I'm a girl. I was surprised how frustrated I became. I asked myself, how dare he assume and question my ability? How dare he see me as less than a man? It was hard to think someone could say these things about me without even giving me a chance. This man may not have a direct impact on me and my choices, but experiencing this opened my eyes to the extent of how badly women are discriminated against in the world of percussion. Sure, it's gotten better over the past few years, but the sexism isn't completely gone. I believe that women are powerful, creative, passionate, hardworking, dedicated, and most of all, courageous. We've fought for so long to win equal rights and respect for women, and we've more than proved we're capable of anything we put our minds to. I believe in women empowerment and I believe that we were given a voice to use it for good.

◆ ◆ ◆

STORY NUMBER 36

EILEEN
age: 16 years
New York, USA

My experience is on female education, specifically my experience as a girl who plays percussion, which is largely a male-dominated part of music. Last summer, I was auditioning for From the Top, a program run by NPR that grants scholarships and allows students to perform on the radio. Because I didn't have access to the instrument that I needed at home, I needed to practice and audition at my music school (where I attend a pre-college program during the school year). Because precollege students' ID don't work during the summer, I needed to ask the security guards to let me in manually. On my audition day, when I asked the school's security guard to let me in, he asked me where I was going. After explaining my situation to him and telling him the room number, he looked it up and told me that it did not make sense, as this room was for percussionists, implying that it was clear that I was not a percussion student. Even after politely ensuring him that I did play percussion, he did not believe me until I showed him my mallets, music, and begged him to let me up because my audition was in 10 minutes. Although I usually would not have let microaggressions like this impact me, this experience stuck with me because it occurred in a space where I usually felt safe and respected in. Additionally, I was already nervous for my audition, and this interaction made me angry and uncomfortable. Thinking back on this experience, it felt extremely targeted because there was no point in him doing that: he already knew that I was a precollege student because I showed him my ID, and instead of just accepting the fact that I booked a percussion room, he had to get defensive and question me.

◆ ◆ ◆

STORY NUMBER 37

AMELIA*
age: 13 years
Maharashtra, India

One night my school teacher had called 4 of my friends and i out of our room because we were making too much noise. she sent us to one of the camp instructors rooms to be "reprimanded" or "punished". While there we were sexually, verbally and physically abused. I tried calling for help but we were locked in their room, without any means of contacting anybody in a position of authority. Eventually he left us alone for a few moments, in which time i used the room's phone to call my school PE teacher's room (she was the person in charge of our room) and quickly ran her through the situation. Within moments she got us out. The individual was fired as soon as we returned to the school, but the school was unwilling to let go of the organization because they had been partners for over 20 years. Out of the five girls involved in this incident, including myself, two were twins, and one girl's mother was reluctant to advocate strongly. Therefore, three families, including mine, fought as vigorously as possible given their limited numbers, and eventually, with much effort, succeeded in having the agency fired. Other parents were somewhat more apprehensive about challenging the organization, fearing potential repercussions on how the school might treat their child. However, since I had already planned to leave the school, my family took a very assertive approach to the entire situation. After many sleepless nights, I have mostly recovered from the situation, but my friends still aren't the same people they were before.

◆ ◆ ◆

STORY NUMBER 38

BHUMI
age: 20 years
Chattisgarh, India

My birth name was Bhupendra Das Manikpuri and I was born and raised in New Raipur, Banjari, Chhattisgarh. I was born in the body of a boy but since childhood, I always felt like a girl. My actions were like those of a girl and I was always attracted to boys. It kept going on like this and no one said anything in my childhood. But as soon as I turned 10, I started feeling like a girl trapped in a boy's body. So, I told my mother about how I felt. But, I didn't tell my father since I was scared that he would verbally or physically abuse me. My mother told me to wait for now and that we would find a "solution" in the future. She believed that we should visit a doctor so they could give medicines to "remove" the condition. In India, in Chhattisgarh, in the village area, there was a lot of superstition and she believed that they could do "jadu tona" (witchcraft) to get rid of this "condition." But I wanted to stay away from that even though my mother insisted. I was verbally and physically abused for refusing. Eventually, my mother took me to the doctor, who said he needed to do a blood test as well as hormone test. However I told them that my hormones were fine but my mind believes that I am a girl. I asked the doctor if he could change how I felt in my mind and he said no. So I asked what the point of a hormone test was when he was unable to change how I feel. Later, when I was 15 years old, whilst searching on YouTube, I found out about a boy who surgically transitioned to a girl after surgery. After I saw this video, I tried to find more details. I saw many videos, then I got to know the word "transgender" which meant male to female and female to male. The journey shared by this transwoman on YouTube made me realize I was transgender too. Some time later, I showed my mother the video. Since she is not very educated, she couldn't comprehend what I was telling her. She thought after surgery, I would stay a boy. I reexplained to her but she still didn't understand. I then told her that I was like the people who danced on trains. She started crying and saying I could not be intersex. I then tried to explain to her that I was not intersex but transgender. My mother then requested me to not do anything to bring disgrace to the family or lowly jobs like dancing on trains. She asked me to stay with her and they would support me. However, living with them, we would get into fights sometimes within the family since my brothers could not accept I was transgender. They didn't make any attempt to understand. I had to fight a lot of battles within the family to stand up for myself. My father used to work with the government but got paralyzed. So, he started drinking a lot and passed away in when I was 15. I had to take on his responsibilities but would be verbally abused at work too. When I was 19, I decided to leave home. Through my research on YouTube, I found out about Garima Greh, a shelter home for transgender people and got to know about its local presence in Chhattisgarh. After moving into the home, I stopped calling my mother. It's at that time that she started slowly realizing that she had hurt my feelings very badly and since nobody was fulfilling my dad's work responsibilities, she realized what she was missing. She told me that she was accepting me for who I was and encouraged me to be myself and not let anyone treat me badly. That day I decided to take on a job I was proud of. I have now applied for a vacancy in the Chhattisgarh police and I am preparing for that job. I am now living in this shelter home with other transgender people like me and I feel very comfortable, something I never felt in my village. And after coming here, my mind feels so different. Earlier, I used to feel depressed. That has now improved. I have a counselor, who has helped me deal with my depression. I now want to be open with my story and tell the whole world about my journey.

(translated from Hindi audio to English text)

◆ ◆ ◆

STORY NUMBER 39

SIDDHI "SAKSHI"
age: 22 years
Chattisgarh, India

My name used to be Siddhant Nage and I have now officially changed it to Siddhi "Sakshi" Nage. I am from Jagdalpur city in the Bastar district in Chhattisgarh. I have been living in a shelter home for transgender people for the last three and a half years. I was born in a male body and my family thought that I was a boy. Up to age 10, I did not know what I was. I lived like a normal boy. But my way of living was different. I liked to play with dolls. Boys played with bikes, cars, and cricket. I did not have any interest in that. I did not have any interest in boys' games. When I was 10 years old, I started noticing the differences. When I used to see sarees or make-up, I used to feel like wearing them. But my family did not support me. My father used to hate it. He thought I was destroying my life. At home, I used to take my mother's sarees and bangles, and my sister's make-up, go to a separate room at midnight, close the door and secretly try them on, making sure no one at home or outside could see me. My school life was very difficult. The teachers and students used to torture me. They used to call me "chhakka" (derogatory word for intersex people) in 6th grade. They used to call me gay when I was in 9th grade and made me stay away from them since I was different. The teachers and students alike would laugh at me. The boys would pull my pants down to check whether I was male or female or lock me in the bathroom. They would tear my shirt or tear pages in my book. The teachers would ridicule my clothes. Nobody would sit with me since I was different. Consequently, I dropped out after finishing

11th grade since I was depressed. I was tense because I didn't know myself. On top of that, people verbally or physically abused me. If I told my family or school, they would blame me. Everything was negative for me. So, I decided to take stock of my life and managed to get a job in room service at a hotel. However, the managers and guests of the hotel also eventually verbally or sexually abused me. I somehow managed to work there with great difficulty for 6 months and then used the money to buy a phone. The first thing I learnt by browsing the web on this phone was what LGBTQ meant. Until I had this phone, I didn't know myself. Was I a man, a woman, trans, gay? I didn't know. The day I got the phone, I searched on YouTube what boy-boy love was. I searched a lot. I used to search on Google every day about boys not interested in girls. I did always want a husband and family even if I couldn't have kids biologically. But I could get a surgery and live a good life. I knew then I was a transwoman. Then I downloaded the Grindr app. There was a lot of dating on it. But then I found a boy and was in a relationship with him for 7 years. He was from Bhanupratapur. Initially my family didn't realize what it was and thought he was a friend. I would visit him at his home too. Then I decided I wanted to live with him forever. When his family got to know, they got very upset and verbally abused both of us. I came back home and stopped talking to him. And then I was depressed for 12 months and couldn't eat or do anything because of that. So I joined a "Kinnar" (intersex and transgender) group against my family's wishes. My father came to pick me up a few times and even filed a police report but I continued staying with them. But, they tortured me there as well. I was physically abused and they would force me to beg and work as a sex worker. Then my mother got sick so I came home. But some of the transgender people came to my house and started beating me up. They even threatened my parents so I ran away and hid out for 2-3 days without eating or drinking. After that, the news spread in my village that I was transgender so I didn't know where to go. I was alone. I contacted my transgender friend who informed me that there was a vacancy in Bastar Fighters (police). So I moved to Raipur into the hostel.

After living there for two years, I got a job as a security guard at a company called Vedanta Limited Company in Jhansuguda. I was very happy. I was very happy because I was getting a job with my identity. I lived well for two months. After that, gradually people started asking me why I dressed differently and acted differently. One night a man came into my room and tried to force himself on me but I somehow ran away. I went back into depression and returned home. My mother was fine but my father looked at me angrily and asked me why I dressed like a woman or grew my hair. He yelled at my mother and physically abused her for me being transgender. I was the first person in Bastar with official documents stating I am transgender. The collector helped me with this transition very quickly and I was able to change my sex officially in a month. This gave me a lot of courage. I have now been preparing for a police constable job for the last 7 months. And my hope is that once I get a job, my life will change. Thanks to Garima Greh, transgender people have had a chance to live in Chhattisgarh. To make things better for us, we, as a society, need to provide education about transgender people at schools so children grow up understanding, accepting and respecting us.

(translated from Hindi audio to English text)

◆ ◆ ◆

STORY NUMBER 40

SABURI
age: 26 years
Chhatisgarh, India

My name is Saburi Shankar Yadav and I am a transgender woman. My parents named me Shankar Yadav. I'm 26 years old. I was born and brought up in Korba, Chhattisgarh. When I was in school, I felt different from other boys. I also felt uncomfortable when they would talk about girls. But, I really enjoyed talking to girls and being friends with them. I was definitely more comfortable with girls. When they would talk about boys, I would enjoy that too. When I turned 13, I realized that was different from other people and I liked to live like girls do. There was a lot of stigma and discrimination in school life. Literally, because of my activities and because I was "girlish", the other students would make fun of me and discriminate. I had to be very deliberate about what time I went to the bathroom since I had to use the boys' bathroom. When I would go to the bathroom, I used to see that people were looking at me in a weird way or commenting on me. So, it was a big challenge for me to even go to the bathroom. When I was in 8th grade, 4-5 of the seniors at school came into the bathroom, pulled my clothes and locked me in the bathroom. I was locked in a 3 x 3 space for 40 minutes. One of the cleaners finally came and opened the door. When asked why I was in there, I was not in a situation to say anything. After that day, I didn't have the courage to go back to school. After the 2nd or 3rd day, when I went back to school and told my teacher about the incident, she said it was my fault and I brought it upon myself because I behaved like girls did. After that, I didn't have the courage to go back to school so I dropped out after 8th grade. I studied from 9th-12th grade privately. I also did private college education and graduated successfully. In high school, I studied science, sociology, economics and also Hindi literature in college. I went on to work at an NGO. I became very interested in the social sectors. I wanted to do social work. I wanted to partake in activism. I wanted to work for people like me. I wanted to become a trans activist. The beginning of my police journey was in 2017. There are great trans activists in Chhattisgarh namely Vidya Rajput and Raveena

Bareeha who did a lot of activism and spread awareness, sensitization programs, etc and created options for trans people in government jobs. Chhattisgarh was the first state in India which gave options to direct transgenders in government jobs. Then, a column appeared in the police department for trans people. So, there were jobs for male, female as well as transgender people. So, at that time in 2017, I applied for the job and Vidya let me stay with her to prepare for the exam. I cleared the physical exam, but the written exam was a bigger challenge for the trans people since our education had been severely affected due to the discrimination. So, we needed a boost compared to others. Our trans activists like Vidya and Raveena wrote a letter to the ministry to let us stay in the administration academy for a month to prepare for the written test. But, after that month, we needed a place to continue staying at. So, the social welfare department had a building where we stayed and prepared for the test for 6 months. There were about 20 people living there and different teachers used to visit and tutor us on different subjects. We used to get up at 6 am, freshen up and sit for classes at 9 am. Class used to be from 9 to 1. From 1 to 2, we would have lunch and rest. Then we used to study again at 5 pm and then dinner from 8 to 9. From 9 pm to 11 pm we used to study and then off to bed. This was our schedule at that time. After all this effort, we took the written test. However, then the elections happened, and the government changed and the police jobs for us were paused. It was a huge setback for us for which we had given almost a year of our lives. Then, COVID came. And the police jobs pause for us continued until 2021 when the government came back and said that we would need to clear the physical test again. It had been 3 years since the last one. They had updated the tests and was disadvantageous for trans people in India since due to the discrimination, we had never been able to pursue any athletic goals actively. Nevertheless we took the exam and on 30th March, 2021, we got the results. 13 were able to successfully clear the test and I was one of them! After that, we went to police training school where we were trained physically and mentally. We had classes ranging from the constitution, criminology, computers and English language. We were treated very well during training by the staff and teachers. In 2017, when we were preparing for the police, New York Times journalists came to shoot a documentary on us. That was an awesome moment in my life. But since the government changed, the documentary could not be made which was very disappointing. I have now been in this job for about 3 years. While reactions to us being in police jobs have been mixed, I have seen the transition and now people appreciate us being in these jobs. Other transgender people look at us as an inspiration for what they could be. Today, when I talk to transgender people, they say that they feel proud to see me and they want to become like me. So, it is a big thing for me that I am able to inspire others. And especially that I am able to help a community that may not even be considered by their family. This is a big achievement for me.

(translated from Hindi audio to English text)

◆ ◆ ◆

STORY NUMBER 41

HANNAH
age: 18 years
New York, USA

As a female in debate, a predominately male activity, I've had to struggle with finding my voice and finding my place. That's why I hosted Horace Manns gender in debate conference this year where we invited speakers and held workshop sessions about gender inequality.

◆ ◆ ◆

STORY NUMBER 42

N.P.*
age: 14 years
Maharashtra, India

I was trying to spread awareness, help break the stigma of menstrual hygiene, and promote a sustainable menstrual product by giving a talk about it to the members of my building society. I had planned and prepped for this moment for a long time and had sent out multiple reminders and updates to the society to make sure they would come. In the end there was a grand total of 4 society members who attended the talk which was a bit underwhelming. We did get the female staff members to attend which made a positive impact and difference to them, but it was still disappointing to experience.

◆ ◆ ◆

STORY NUMBER 43

KATE*
age: 14 years
California, USA

For my entire life, the academic environment around me was always hyper competitive. For example, in my elementary and middle school, there was a "best work" board which was saved for only the highest of scorers, and my school had a non-existent athletic and arts program. So the only way students could compare themselves was with grades. The kids with the highest grades were always treated with the utmost respect (by students and teachers alike) and the kids with the lowest grades were often ridiculed by the whole class. This, paired with parental expectations, put me under a lot of pressure from an extremely early age that only increased as I got older. The pressure and need for academic validation got so bad that by the time I was in middle school, my entire self-esteem was based on my grades. It was then that COVID-19 hit. After not having school for basically five whole months, the change of environment that I had to take classes in was like a slap in the face. It was impossible for me to focus on classes when Youtube was just a few keystrokes away. My grades took a big hit, and I lost all motivation to even attend classes anymore. I was failing every test, and somehow even when I cheated on my tests, I would still get subpar grades. Honestly, that time was probably the worst I had felt about myself in my whole life. The isolation combined with my dwindling motivation curbed my self-esteem to an all-time low. I could barely get out of bed and struggled with some really scary thoughts. It slowly got better though. The turning point was finally having a real conversation with my mom. I remember that she told me a lot of stuff that I really needed to hear, like that she knew I was trying my best and, even if I flunked out of high school, she would still love me no matter what. And the next year, when we came back to school in person, I was struggling a lot less and, after a few months, eventually got control back of my grades. I also kept reminding myself that I am so much more than my grades and tried not to put as much emphasis on my academics. I guess the moral of the story is that your self-esteem and view of yourself shouldn't be solely based on achievements or societal expectations. There are some things about ourselves that we can't change and we just have to accept our flaws rather than continually bring ourselves down because of them. If you're ever having a hard time, just talk to someone. You'll be surprised how much a simple conversation can change your perspective and give you some peace. Thanks for listening!

◆ ◆ ◆

STORY NUMBER 44

ISRAT
age: 16 years
Barishal District, Bangladesh

I am an YES (Youth Exchange and Study) Alumni. I completed my exchange year successfully in the U.S. And lived there with a host family. I also went to an U.S. high school. I was placed in Madison, Wisconsin and my school's name was Madison East High. When I got to know that I got selected for this program, I was honestly so excited and couldn't wait to experience new things. The love my host parents gave me is truly unexplainable. They made me feel like home. However, as a 15 year old who had never lived away from their family, it wasn't that easy. Fomo or fear of missing out was a big thing. There were times when I missed my family a lot. There were times when I wished I could just meet my friends from my home country once. It surely affected my mental health. My school was huge! There were so many students. It was a big change for me but I had the ability to get through all this. My adaptability and flexibility helped me a lot. Being an exchange student is definitely hard but it helps you to be strong and independent. It teaches you stuff that you are going to need all your life. It changes your perspective of viewing the world..you become more acceptant towards new cultures and customs. I'm sharing this story so that the people who read it understand that being an exchange student is not a cup of tea, but the memories and the connections you make are forever going to stick with you so it's definitely worth it!

◆ ◆ ◆

STORY NUMBER 45

KAYLA
age: 16 years
Pennsylvania, USA

My freshman year of high school was the rock bottom of my raw sixteen years of life thus far. That summer, my parents had told my brother and me they were getting a divorce. The news absolutely upturned my reality and spun my world around - I'm still spinning, really. Two years later, I continue to feel the magnitude of my parents' separation ripple through my thoughts. It's no easy feat to stomach the idea that my parents, the people who were supposed to be my epitome of happily-ever-after, had fallen out of love.

It's no secret that I was in a vulnerable position that freshman year, following the summer of 2022. It was a time that I was (involuntarily) adjusting to the novel and tender transition into being a child of divorce. It was a time that I was adapting to the idea of no more family dinners, living in two houses, and being away from one parent for a week at once. It was a time that I needed support - support that I was supposed to find in my friends.

Come September, my friend group and I were thriving. I'd always imagined that we'd stick together forever. We'd seen other cliques separate in middle school - but we survived. Surely we'd last. My best friend at the time, R, was my rock. We were an inseparable duo - one that could most definitely brave high school.

I still remember the day that everything fell apart. Freshman year meant parties - real parties. Halloween season arrived, and half of my friend group got invited to said "real party". R was invited. I was not. The part that hurt the most wasn't the invite, rather the fact that I heard of its existence (absence) from hallway talk. Furthermore, nobody - not even R - attempted to get the rest of my group in. It's silly, really, how one stupid invitation to a "cool" party can slice through years of friendship and memories.

From that day forward, R and that seemingly-better half began to hang out with the party group. More and more often, that half of our group would be spotted on SnapMap or other social media platforms with the party group. I refuse to use the term "popular" as a label for the party group. I can recall that after the NYE party, another party that we weren't invited to, we were all sitting at lunch. The party half of my group was talking about their weekend, debriefing on all of the crazy cool stuff we had missed out on. I remember looking across the cafeteria and seeing the party group wave R and the girls over from our table. I can picture how, one by one, R and the girls who were supposed to be my best friends got up and left to sit at the other table. I can feel my heart dropping all over again. Not a single one of them said a word - not in that moment, not later that day, not later that week, and not to this day.

For a while, I held a grudge against them all. How could they have betrayed our group? How could they have just abandoned us - and all without a sorry? I was the most hurt by R. She was the first girl I'd called while crying to tell her about my parents that last summer. I needed her. Sometimes, I still feel like I need her. I felt like I wasn't good enough. Clearly, I didn't meet the "popular" girls' standards to be invited to their parties and then into their group. Clearly, R did. A constant comparison of myself and other girls raged on. I felt like I was constantly missing out - like I deserved to be there. My jealousy turned into judgement of that group. I'd think about the wrong things they were doing - when deep down I wanted those experiences. I would talk about these rumors with the other people who were excluded. Sharing my rage with them felt like the right thing to do. This led to almost all of my friends ostracizing me.

Climbing out of that hole was hard - one of the hardest things I've ever had to do. My therapist, Caroline, has taught me so many lessons, one of which is this: she asked me to pick my three favorite flowers. I selected hydrangeas, roses, and tulips. She then told me to compare them - WHY was one better than the other? When I couldn't produce an answer, she smiled and said, "Exactly. You can't compare the three, because they all are their own unique entities with unique qualities that only they have. People are like that. Don't compare yourself to others when nobody is comparable to anybody else but their self."

That year, while I lost my best friend R, I met my current best friend, S. She brought light and laughter into the rest of my year. I stopped gossiping and started focusing on myself, rather than other people. I reminded myself that others' opinions of me are none of my business. This is not to say that I don't have slip ups, or bad days, or bad weeks. I'm still healing from my parents' separation, and from my best friend leaving me, and from my friend group's splitting. Maybe I always will be - but that doesn't mean that there isn't light at the end of the tunnel, where skies are blue. Skies don't have to be blue all the time - they can't possibly be. But Reader, you will get through your stormy rock-bottoms. Like waves, this too, shall pass :)

◆ ◆ ◆

STORY NUMBER 46

TANYA

age: 12 years
New York, USA

I am lucky to go to a school that provides me good education and support from my family and school. We talk about physical and mental health in health class at school. In case of any problem I know that I can reach out to my teachers and my family to support me.

◆ ◆ ◆

STORY NUMBER 47

A.S.*
age: 19 years
New York, USA

Throughout high school, I have noticed that especially in humanities and participation-based classes, there is a difference between my female peers and me in comparison to my male peers. In particular, male students in my classes tended to be more confident and inclined to share their views in comparison to female students. In fact, a poll taken for my school newspaper showed that this trend was supported by the numbers too. By writing this article, I was able to discover that contrary to popular belief, gender disparities still pervade school classrooms to a significant extent, and a lot of work has to be done to truly eliminate these from our environments.

◆ ◆ ◆

STORY NUMBER 48

ANONYMOUS-2*
age: undisclosed
Barishal District, Bangladesh

Self confidence is something I really struggled with greatly. Whenever I used to look at my reflection, I didn't like my face. I have been dealing with acne for a long time, and for that reason, I didn't like my face. Truth is, it's okay to not like some aspects of our body, but it is important to embrace ourselves because we all are unique in our own way ways. Self-love does not make anyone a selfish person. Rather, it helps to boost one's self confidence. If I don't love myself, no one will do that for me. All I want to say is that we should love who we are, and try to have a positive mindset on our image. Doing self care and loving ourselves can help us feel confident.

◆ ◆ ◆

STORY NUMBER 49

ANONYMOUS-3*
age: undisclosed
Barishal District, Bangladesh

Pretty interesting, isn't it? The journey a little girl has to go through to be a young lady. A lot of girls out there are curious to know that some other girls might be afraid. But at the end of the day, every little girl goes through this journey and turns out to be a beautiful young lady. Generally, every girl goes through similar experiences, but there is also a lot of variety. I will try my best to include those parts of this journey which are similar for every girl. Typically, a girl starts this journey of their life between the ages of 8 to 13. This journey is widely known as "female puberty," or "pubertal development in girls." The stages of this journey include the thelarche, pubarche, and menarche. These three stages are very crucial for us as they ensure our physical and mental development to a great extent. The term "thelarche" refers to the development of our chest. On the other hand, "pubarche" refers to the development of pubic hair, and the term "menarche" refers to the cycle of menstruation. We noticed that "thelarche" and "pubarche" both involve physical development. But, a lot of girls may not know or understand the "menarche" stage. Many might question themselves saying "What is menstruation?" And honestly, you should be, because it is a very, very significant fragment of our life. Now then, what is menstruation actually? What does it do? Is it physical or mental development? How does it affect our health? There might be too many questions on your mind. Let me elaborate on myself. Menstruation is the monthly shedding of the lining of the uterus in females. It is a regular and natural change that occurs in the female reproductive system to make pregnancy possible. In easier terms, menstruation is the monthly discharge of blood and tissue from the uterine lining through the vagina. Now don't get scared because it involves blood. In fact, be proud of yourself and your body because it's capable of discharging blood–that too, monthly. As mentioned before, yes, this is a very important phase of life, as it allows you to get pregnant in the future. So yes, we have to go through this. "Does it hurt?" "How do I stop the bleeding?" "Is there any way to prevent it?" There might be too many questions on your mind again. And once again, let me answer all of them. Yes, it hurts a lot. Like come on, you're bleeding. One thing to keep in mind: it happens for five continuous days for a month. It can be seven to ten days for a few girls. So, that's a relief. And, do not get scared of the bleeding or pain. Seriously. It's nothing to be afraid of. Look at your mom. She gave birth to you. And she went through labor pain. That aside she went through menstruation too. She goes through it every month. You might not even notice it. My point is that every girl goes through this. And honestly, it might sound pretty tough, but it's actually worth it. Besides, you're a brave girl there. You are a strong, beautiful girl who is excited about all of the adventures of life. It's going to be a piece of cake for you. Your motto should be not to be afraid. If you're afraid this might be a challenge. So my suggestion is to take it easy. It's going to be okay. You can't stop the bleeding, nor prevent it. But, you can manage it by following some hygiene and rules. First of all, whenever your period or menstruation starts, use a hygienic product like a pad or something else. It depends on what you're comfortable with. You need to have a healthy diet filled with protein and vitamins. If it hurts too much, you can you can have some painkillers or consult a doctor. And they are your tour guide for your physical concerns. Menstruation also affects you mentally, and this is another reason why it's a vital portion of life. Periods help us by shaping our mentality. I've heard a few people say "Girls get mature through their period." While I surely can't say how much of a truth this is, I can definitely say it affects us mentally. You might go through mood swings, anxiety, fatigue, etc. You might also face sadness or even depression. Cognitive changes are possible too. At this time, you don't know what you might face. So, do not hide it from your parents. They are the ones who will support you through this and help you overcome this difficult period. This is probably how you mature through your period. But again, don't worry and be brave. You got this. You will face many hormonal changes too. But, hormonal changes vary from person to person. Now let's talk about some dark truths related to this. While reading, did it concern you how society may react to this? It may or may concern you, but you have to be careful. In some places, menstruation is considered as a taboo. Yes, they think it's impure and forbids us from doing a lot of things. Society is starting to change its perspective, slowly but surely, and becoming more positive about it. But still, be careful. Not because you will be teased, but because of your sense of your self-respect. You will be surprised, but this common natural phenomenon is not perceived normally. Still, some people get shy while talking about it. Some boys even tease girls about it. But, after all, this is society. These are the challenges you need to face. But, I can assure you, the situation is slowly changing. So, we have got nothing to worry about. But, be careful. I hope I could help all of you by giving you a general idea of what you will go through. I really hope that my lovely young girls out there are helped by this message. Remember that you are going to be alright.

◆ ◆ ◆

STORY NUMBER 50

ANONYMOUS-4*
age: undisclosed
Barishal District, Bangladesh

Girls' health is a crucial aspect of overall societal well-being, encompassing physical, mental and emotional dimensions. During childhood and adolescence, girls undergo significant developmental changes that require proper nutrition, physical activity and health care. Access to education and health information empowers them to make informed choices about their bodies and future. Additionally, mental health support is vital as girls navigate the challenges of growing up facing pressures from academic, social and sometimes familiar expectations. Ensuring girls have a safe environment free from violence and discrimination is essential for their healthy development. By addressing these needs comprehensively, society can foster a generation of healthy, confident and capable women.

◆ ◆ ◆

STORY NUMBER 51

SHARABAN
age: undisclosed
Barishal DISTRICT, Bangladesh

Growing up, I always excelled in school. Education was my escape, a realm where I felt confident and capable. However, my journey wasn't always smooth. When I was in grade 5, I had to change schools and move to a new one for grade 6. The transition was challenging. I struggled to study, communicate with others, and fit in with my new classmates. During my time in school, I also had to endure a lot of bad comments about my height and weight. These hurtful remarks affected my self esteem and made it even harder to focus on my studies. On top of that, I was dealing with some personal issues at home, which added to the stress and made concentration on schoolwork difficult. By the time I reached high school, I started to struggle with several anxiety. The pressure to maintain high grades combined with the expectations of my teachers and parents began to take a toll on my mental health. I remember the night spent staring at my textbooks and notes, unable to concentrate because of my overwhelming fear of failure. My anxiety manifested physically too. I experienced frequent headaches, body pain and stomach aches. Despite these challenges, I was reluctant to seek help, fearing it would be seen as a sign of weakness. One day I decided to talk about these with one of my friends. She encouraged me to talk to the school counselor, who helped me understand that my mental health was just as important as my academic achievements. With her support, I learned coping strategies to manage my anxiety and gradually found a balance between my studies and self care. Sharing my story with other girls who might be going through similar experiences is important to me. I want them to know that it's okay to seek help and prioritize their mental health. Education is vital and so is our well-being. By taking care of ourselves, we can truly thrive and reach our potential our full potential. Thank you.

◆ ◆ ◆

STORY NUMBER 52

ANONYMOUS-5*
age: undisclosed
Barishal District, Bangladesh

Finding My Own Way to Balance: Starting high school was exciting, but also a bit overwhelming. Even though I stayed at the same school, I still felt a lot of pressure to do well in my classes and keep up with everything. The stress from school made me feel anxious, and sometimes it was hard for me to sleep or concentrate. And I never talked to my parents or teachers about how I was feeling. Instead, I tried to find my own way to manage the stress. One thing that really helped me was keeping a journal notebook. Writing down my thoughts and feelings made my worries seem smaller and help me understand what was bothering me. Another big thing that helped me was spending time on my hobbies. I used to do crafting, which I like the most. And I also liked reading books and collecting some flowers. I enjoyed doing those things. It was like taking a little break from all the stress. When things felt too overwhelming, I would take a short break to do something fun and to have some fun. For example, I would listen to music, go to the rooftop, or take a walk. These breaks helped me clear my mind and tackle everything. I also learned to be kinder to myself and think about myself. Instead of always pushing for perfect grades, I started setting realistic goals and reminding myself that it's okay not to be perfect. Nobody is perfect. Perfect in the world. There are things I can do that other people can't. Everyone has a talent. Although I didn't do group study with my friends, I felt comfortable spending time with them. To any girl who may feel the same way, remember that it's okay to find your own way to feel better. You don't have to go through this alone, even if you handle things differently. Find activities that make you feel happy and be kind to yourself. And be self-dependent. You are stronger than you think. Study hard and focus on your goals. One day you're gonna make yourself proud. Remember that believing in yourself vs being overconfident are different!

◆ ◆ ◆

STORY NUMBER 53

AFRIN
age: undisclosed
Barishal District, Bangladesh

Throughout my educational journey, I have faced numerous challenges that have significantly impacted my mental and physical health. From a young age, the pressure to excel academically was immense, leading to high levels of stress and anxiety. Balancing school work with personal life often felt overwhelming, and there were times when I doubted my abilities and questioned my self worth. The constant need to meet led to sleepless nights, constant fatigue and bouts of anxiety that made it difficult to focus and perform at my best. However, reaching out to other girls who shared similar experiences provided a sense of comfort and solidarity. Engaging in heartfelt conversations about our struggles and triumphs had me realize that I was not alone in my journey. It fostered a supportive community where we could openly discuss our mental health and educational challenges without fear of judgment. These interactions were crucial in promoting resilience and a positive mindset. We exchanged tips on managing stress, coping strategies and even study techniques that helped us stay on track. By sharing our stories, we uplifted each other, offering encouragement, empathy and practical advice. This camaraderie not only alleviated my stress, but also motivated me to persevere and strive for excellence. I believe that sharing our experiences can inspire and support other girls facing similar difficulties, helping them navigate their own paths with greater confidence and strength. Together, we can create a network of empowerment, fostering a generation of young women who are resilient, compassionate and successful despite the obstacles they encounter. Moreover, these connections have taught me the value of vulnerability and the strength that comes from community support, knowing that there are others who understand and share my struggles. This has encouraged me to be more open about my feelings and seek help when needed, rather than suffering in silence. In summary, my educational journey, though fraught with challenges, has been greatly enriched by the support of a community of like minded girls. Our shared experiences have not only helped us cope with the pressures of academic life, but have also empowered us to face future challenges with courage and resilience. By continuing share out stories, we can extend this support to even more girls, helping uplift and inspired them on their own journeys.

◆ ◆ ◆

STORY NUMBER 54

SAPTO
age: undisclosed
Barishal DISTRICT, Bangladesh

Like other girls in the world, I also faced challenges in our school. Whether physical or mental health difficulties, problems are a part of life and must be taken as obstacles to success. Uneasiness is a regular part of school life. It's a feeling that can never be fully experienced to someone outside our educational boundaries. No matter how many friends you have, you will sometimes feel lonely as a girl. Girls are always dealing with things on their own, staring at the ceiling. They endure the inner pain and insecurity they face. There are countless stories of the difficulties I faced, but nowadays I tend to ignore them and just go with the flow. As a girl, I was always judged by the way I sit, dress, and walk. You might end up being the laughing stock of the senior girls if you walk a little clumsily. People giggle in the most unexpected way. Girls face things like this all the time. All my life, I felt like everyone was my enemy because they look at my tiny flaws rather than my polished talent. The whole world feels like a judicial court. At times, I feel so much hatred from this world. it feels like being in a competition without even meaning to. I suffered from depression under all those judgmental stares, always fearing that I would become the laughing stock at school or the topic of gossip for minor flaws. But, the world isn't as bad as you think. It seems like it's full of wonder. If you look beyond the judgments and embrace your true self, you can embrace the essence of education and find beauty in the opportunities it offers. Our mental health plays a crucial role in keeping us balanced, so as long as you know how to appreciate it, the inner turmoil will feel so small. Delving deeper into my studies, I have been taught to ignore this judgment and tiny flaws in shaping my light of teaching. Being inspired by small things in nature will earn every girl and young woman a bright future ahead. I have a feeling this is relatable to many.

◆ ◆ ◆

STORY NUMBER 55

ANONYMOUS-6*
age: undisclosed
Barishal District, Bangladesh

As a teenage girl, I find that balancing mental and physical health is crucial for my overall well being. Physically taking care of myself involves regular exercise, nutritious eating habits and sufficient sleep. Engaging in activities like yoga or running not only keeps me fit, but also helps alleviate stress and boost my mood. Eating a balanced diet ensures that I have the energy I need throughout the day, while adequate sleep allows my body to recharge and recover. Mentally, navigating through adolescence can be challenging. I prioritize my mental health by practicing mindfulness and relaxation techniques. These help me manage stress and anxiety that often accompany academic and social pressures. Journaling has become a helpful outlet for expressing my emotions and processing my thoughts. Additionally, seeking support from trusted friends and family members provides me with a sense of belonging and comfort during difficult times. Finding a balance between physical and mental health is a continuous journey. By listening to my body, and acknowledging my emotions, I empower myself to make choices that promote overall wellness. This approach not only enhances my daily life, but also prepares me for the challenges and opportunities that lie ahead in adulthood.

◆ ◆ ◆

STORY NUMBER 56

ANAN
age: undisclosed
Barishal District, Bangladesh

During the time I started high school, I tackled a lot of mental health issues that impacted my academic life. There was mental pressure to achieve the highest grades in exams. Feeling pressured to maintain all of the things made it really really hard for me to concentrate on my studies because I used to overthink and lack confidence. A bunch of negative feelings were attached to my mental health including overthinking, nervousness, lack of confidence, and a fear of being judged. At this time, I lost my confidence to ask people for help. My fear of being judged prevented me from taking part in many things, which was very heartbreaking. Eventually, I tried to think out of the box, I tried to talk with myself rather than talking with others. I told myself "You're so perfect. What's lacking you behind?" There was just one thing that you are lacking: communication to yourself, but you just did that today. Bravo! The mind of positiveness is opening tomorrow. It's the time to say goodbye to all of the negative and intrusive thoughts you had on your mind. I'm really proud of you, myself. Then my confidence level increased rapidly. I realized that, now, nothing can stop me from achieving the highest grades. In conclusion, sometimes we girls think that if we talk about our mental stress with someone else, then we will be fine. This way is right. But on the other hand, what if we think to communicate with ourselves? Remember one thing: you are the best friend of yourself. No one can understand you the way you do to yourself.

So, talk to yourself! Let's motivate yourself to make the best version of you. Show everyone that hidden gem inside you. Be the confident you.

◆ ◆ ◆

STORY NUMBER 57

AYESHA
age: undisclosed
Barishal District, Bangladesh

I, Ayesha Anwar, am a student of grade 9 from the Jahanara Israil School & College. In this article I would like to share how my experience with education affected my mental and physical health. Growing up in a small town education was both a beacon of hope and a source of pressure for me. Being girl in a community where expectations were often limited by traditional roles, pursuing academic excellence was a double edged sword. I loved learning, but it came with challenges. In high school, I've thrown myself into my studies, aiming to prove that I can do something. The pressure to perform perfectly took a toll on my mental health. I struggled with anxiety and perfectionism, constantly feeling like I needed to meet unrealistic standards set by myself and others. It affected my sleep, my social life and even my physical health. There were days when I questioned whether pushing myself so hard was healthy. But then there were moments of triumph–acing a tough exam or receiving recognition for my achievement–that reminded me why I persisted. Through it all, I found support and unexpected places like teachers who believed in me and eventually a community of like minded individuals online, who shared similar experiences. Connecting with different people who are navigating the same challenges helped me realize that I was not alone. Education shaped not just my knowledge but also my resilience. It taught me to balance ambition with self care, to seek help when needed and to read and find success on my own terms. Today, I advocate for mental health awareness and support system to inspire others.

◆ ◆ ◆

STORY NUMBER 58

ANSHA
age: undisclosed
Barishal District, Bangladesh

Leave it to the Future: I, Ansha Tajrian, have been very indecisive about my future plans. It seems as though every year, I get a new aim in life. Sometimes, I want to be a doctor, sometimes I want to be a scientist. Other times I want to be a detective or a journalist or study archeology or history. I want to try everything, but I know I should choose one profession. I'm so indecisive about my future. Often times I feel insecure and anxious because everyone around me seems to have it all planned out. Everyone seems to have their future goals fixed and they know exactly what to do. Whenever someone asks me, "What's your aim in life?" I don't know what to say. I often lie because I'm too scared that if I say "I don't know," I might get shamed for it. But then I saw my friend with similar issues as me. But, she isn't too anxious about it. According to her, we are still so young. We have a long way ahead before we enter the professional world. Even if we have everything planned out, who's to say that we will be able to do things according to the plan? We could have one dream now, but we might end up doing something completely different. It's okay if you don't have a set goal now. What matters is that you wish to do something in the future. You want to find your purpose. And what might that be? Let the future decide! I'm still in grade nine, my life has just begun. If one worries about their future too much, they will forget to live in the present. Let the future decide itself.

◆ ◆ ◆

STORY NUMBER 59

RABIA
age: undisclosed
Barishal District, Bangladesh

A Teenager's Identity Crisis: Is it even possible to feel superior & inferior at the same time? Is it possible to feel like you are so many people at once? Is it possible to be visible yet invisible at times? Well, yes. Something I have often heard from my mom is "Being a teenager is like being on a roller coaster of emotions. At times you feel like you are at the zenith, and then you feel like nothing more than a sand particle that has fallen apart." During the initial days of my teenage years, I thought there was no way this entire teenage-emotions "blah, blah, blah" thing would reach me. I was so confident, probably because of my blind faith and my sophistication. However, every dot of my mom's words started to connect as soon as I reached my actual teenage years. I have found myself in such a scenario where I'm standing amidst feeling invincible but not being able to measure up. Somewhere in the middle, people believe in my academic excellence. At some points, I do too. But mostly, I feel that whatever goodness I have achieved in my academics so far is not yet worthy of being called excellent, invincible, or simply the best. In this regard, my friends have always managed to flatter me, complimenting me in every possible way. However, deep in my heart, I know that there is a lot missing. But what? Apart from academics, numerous experiences have contributed to my identity crisis. As a student involved more or less in debates, anchoring, speeches, and various competitions, the expectations placed upon me, if I am not wrong, have always been high. My teachers, parents, and friends have/do/will always expect the best for me from me. I definitely expect the same as well, but not knowing why, I feel hollow sometimes. I feel numb sometimes. Why do I sometimes feel like all the expectations placed upon me might only lead to a destination of disappointment? Why do I have this terrible fear of being good at first and then faltering when the actual test arrives? And how come I mostly manage to hide or conceal it? It's not that every time I have felt disappointed or unsatisfied with my work. On the contrary, I obviously have my own achievements that I can't help being proud of. But in some cases, when I had a great deal of expectations and eyes upon me, sometimes tangled with tension and pressure, I had successfully managed to mess up. This is what truly worries me: Am I genuinely good, or is it just a mirage of people? Or perhaps, are my own false perceptions and self-doubts obscuring my view? Yet another significant aspect of my life where I couldn't decide who I am is my relationships and communication with people. They are so diverse that I feel as if I am a mosaic of too many personalities. Some might say that this is indeed normal. But somehow I just can't digest it. In my professional life, i.e. school, I usually manage to interact with people wisely and responsibly. With my buddies. I'm friendly. Let's say that I'm ambivert there. Whereas at home, I'm an absolutely different person. I probably don't even speak more than 100 words a day there. It's not that I don't share a strong bond with my family, but still, why can't I interact with them efficiently? And again, when I'm in front of my relatives, whom I always seen growing up now, I usually don't even speak more than 50 words to them. Is it because I'm a child, because I'm an introvert, or because I don't want to be the center of attention? Or is it because I just prioritize my inner peace more? Sometimes I feel that being the youngest, if I speak more, people might think I'm arrogant, but honestly, staying quiet and being a quiet girl isn't promising either. It becomes terrible at times in fact. It feels as if you're strangling your inner voice and letting people stay with whatever perceptions they want to have about you, being clueless about who you really are. While I think this is terrible, I believe it's worth it for my inner peace. Yet again, sometimes I can't help but ponder how astonishingly this has rendered me invisible, muted, and self-centered in the eyes of my own people. But if I prefer staying quiet and unbothered in front of them, how come I manage to interact well enough with people whom I barely know in my professional life? Wasn't it supposed to be the opposite? Anyways, interactions don't help me either. I just find myself being a people pleaser, trying my best to avoid conflicts and disagreements, putting on a good smile while my soul seeks even the tiniest dint of opportunity to speak up about whatever I actually think, believe, and want to say, regardless of others' judgments. Well, it happens very rarely that I speak my heart out. And those bare minimum times when I have done it, I have successfully regretted it later. Probably my inner peace wants to win badly, at any cost. When it comes to my friends, I basically love them. I love my besties and close friends. Usually, I fail to show it. I really wonder what sort of friend I am. Some say that I am understanding; some believe I am mean and selfish; some feel that I care about nothing but my academics; some say I am intelligent, and some simply express that I am boring and reactionless. The funniest part is that I cannot really conclude if any of these characteristics do not exist in me. If I were an element, these characteristics would probably be my isotypes, existing in various percentages that keep changing. Well, I believe that these diverse personalities of mine depend on people's behavior toward me. Rapid changes are possible even due to their tiniest actions. But while these frequent changes happen in "how I appear in front of them," did I somehow lose, or am I losing my real identity? Who am I? Am I the one that people think I am? Or the one they expect me to be? Or am I the one I think I am? And then what on earth do I actually think I am? Most importantly, what is my purpose to serve? What difference can I make? Fun fact: I probably do not even want to know the answers to all these questions right now. I would rather love to know these answers gradually, while connecting every single dot of my identical confusion, placing every irrelevant puzzle piece into a picture. Perhaps. that is how the journey of self-discovery is meant to be. But how do I suppress the storm between my thoughts and actions?

◆ ◆ ◆

STORY NUMBER 60

SARINA
age: 16 years
New York, USA

During my time helping to organize a conference on gender inequality, I was profoundly impacted by the experiences and perspectives shared by our diverse speakers. Our conference brought together speakers, ambassadors and students from various countries whom shed light on how gender norms are portrayed across different cultures, which offered not only me, but the other students attending the conference about how gender norms are represented through different countries and how young students like ourselves can take action. For me, obe of the most inspiring parts of the conference was witnessing student-led debates. Young boys and girls came together to discuss their personal experiences with gender inequality and shared their visions for change. Their passion and determination to fight for gender rights were truly uplifting. It was incredible to see the next generation so committed to making a difference, and it renewed my own commitment to this cause. This experience not only educated me on the complexities of gender inequality but also gave me hope that real, positive change is possible when we all work together. Before attending this conference, I felt like my views and perspectives were so limited to the people around me and what was happening locally, but after I felt like there was so much more to know about and the implications of gender inequality globally, and how some thing that may work in one place may not have the same impact on another place. It was truly inspiring to work with such likeminded people, who shared the same goal, to make the world a more equal and fair place for all genders.

◆ ◆ ◆

STORY NUMBER 61

PIGEON-2*
age: 19 years
Guadalajara, Jalisco, Mexico

Anecdote: Between Darkness and Light I was eight years old when school stopped being a safe place for me. What was supposed to be a space for learning and friendship turned into a daily nightmare. It wasn't that I didn't want to study; I loved learning, but my classmates made me feel as if I were invisible. I was the girl everyone ignored, the one left out of games and conversations. Every day, I wondered what I had done to deserve so much disdain, but the reality is that sometimes, there's no answer. I was just there, and that seemed to be enough for them to hurt me. The worst part was that whenever I tried to defend myself, the teachers always blamed me. It was as if, being a girl, my voice didn't matter. As if my tears didn't matter, and my pain was just an echo in an endless void. The day I finished elementary school, I felt a bitter mix of relief and pain. I had won first place, but at the graduation ceremony, they didn't mention my name. While other girls and boys received their diplomas with smiles and applause, I stood in silence, wondering if I even existed. My mother, who had always been by my side, looked at me with sadness as we left. It wasn't until we were in the parking lot that a teacher caught up with us, handing my mom a crumpled diploma, as if my effort was worth no more than a forgotten piece of paper. The disappointment in my mother's eyes broke my heart. I knew my dad worked tirelessly to make sure we didn't lack anything, and I wanted to be worthy of his sacrifice. But every day was a battle. I hated school, I hated feeling inadequate, I hated the image I saw in the mirror, which only reflected a broken and rejected girl. Over time, that pain rooted itself in my mind, corroding every corner of my self-esteem. I grew up full of self-hatred, convinced that I was worthless. That hatred became a burden so heavy it almost drowned me. Until one day, years later, my mother and I visited an aunt who had returned to the city. That's when I found out that my cousin, someone I had loved like a sister, had taken her own life. The bullying she had suffered at her school was so brutal that she couldn't bear it. Some girls, who felt powerful in destroying her, ripped out chunks of her hair, burned her, and pushed her until she couldn't take it anymore. And then, she decided that death was her only way out. Seeing my aunt devastated, shattered into a thousand pieces, made me realize something I had never considered before: the pain I felt didn't just hurt me; it also had the power to destroy those who loved me. I didn't want to see my mother the way I saw my aunt that day. I couldn't let the darkness I felt in my heart consume me to the point of leading me down the same path. At that time, I was thirteen years old and in middle school. Days after visiting my aunt, one of the girls who had bullied me for years ruined my work by pouring water over it. It was as if she was telling me that I didn't deserve anything good in life. In a fit of desperation and rage, I confronted her. I grabbed her by the hair, threw her to the ground, and poured paint on her face. I screamed that I was tired of her, that it wasn't my fault her parents didn't love her, that it wasn't my fault her mother believed she had ruined their lives. I told her she had no right to make me feel like I was the one who was worthless. She started to cry, and for a brief moment, I felt powerful. But that feeling quickly faded, leaving only an even bigger void than before. I knew what I had done was wrong, but at that moment, it seemed like the only way to make the pain stop. Today, looking back, I realize that even though I got her to stop bothering me, what I really lost was a part of myself. Instead of healing, I filled myself with more hatred, not only towards others but also towards myself for having let anger take over. I learned that violence, whether physical or emotional, only perpetuates the cycle of suffering. Bullying is not just a series of cruel acts; it's a poison that spreads, affecting everyone it touches. My story is a warning to other girls who, in their pain, may be tempted to respond with hatred. Don't let the poison consume you. Seek help, talk to someone who understands you, and above all, never lose hope that things can get better. Because in the end, the real victory is not in defeating those who hurt you, but in finding the strength to love yourself, even when everything else seems to be falling apart.

◆ ◆ ◆

STORY NUMBER 62

MOMO*
age: 20 years
Uganda

Finding Strength in Education and Health: My name is ******* and I grew up in a small village in Uganda. From a young age, I was passionate about learning, but the journey was filled with challenges. My family faced financial difficulties, and many in my community believed that girls didn't need an education. Despite these obstacles, I was determined to pursue my dreams. Every morning, I would wake up early to help my mother with household chores before walking several kilometers to school. The journey was long and tiring, but my love for learning kept me going. At school, I found a sanctuary where I could immerse myself in books and knowledge. However, the pressure of balancing schoolwork and household responsibilities began to take a toll on my mental health. I often felt overwhelmed and anxious, unsure of how to cope with the stress. It was during this time that I attended a health awareness workshop organized by a local NGO. The workshop focused on mental health and self-care, and it was a turning point in my life. I learned that taking care of my mental health was just as important as my physical health. I started practicing mindfulness and self-care techniques, which helped me manage my stress and anxiety. This newfound knowledge empowered me to take control of my well-being and continue pursuing my education with renewed vigor. Inspired by my experiences, I decided to start a girls' empowerment club at my school. The club became a safe space where girls could share their challenges, support each other, and learn about health and education. We organized workshops on mental health, self-care, and academic skills, helping each other grow and thrive.

Through hard work and perseverance, I earned a scholarship to attend a school in the city. This opportunity opened doors I had never imagined. I excelled academically and I am now involved in various initiatives focused on girls' education and mental health. My journey has taught me the importance of resilience, self-care, and community support. I have learned that with determination and the right support, we can overcome any obstacle. Together, we can create a world where every girl has the opportunity to shine and make a difference. This is my story, and I hope it inspires you to keep fighting for what you believe in. Thanks

◆ ◆ ◆

STORY NUMBER 63

LJUBICA
age: 26 years
Pichincha, Quito, Ecuador

Title: The pain that changed my life.

My name is Ljubica, I´m a young, diverse, woman from Ecuador. 2 years ago I started my own Foundation as a memory of my surviving in higher education. From 2015 to 2022 I suffered from political persecution, gender-based discrimination and sexual harassment in my university classrooms by my professors and peers. All because I was a woman and a feminist. My story, unfortunately, is the one faced by many young women in LATAM. We live constantly terrified of how our professors, teachers, mentors, may tomorrow be our abusers and, due to the justice system and ignorance of this problem, today I raise my voice for a pandemic that costs many of us our professional dream. I want to begin this narrative by acknowledging the privilege I had to go all the way to third level education. I am not unaware that in my country and my region, dreaming of being a professional woman is unthinkable for a painful amount of the population. However, I believe, without a doubt, that this is one of the reasons why when we arrive, we do anything to survive... even to die in silence. When I started my university career I can say without a doubt that I was sure that my life had begun. I had too many dreams, goals, ideas of what professional life was going to do for me. However, the first day of my first semester I was surprised by how many times I had to listen to my professors question whether women should be in the classroom and not raising our children. "You don't come here to find a husband!" was the first thing they warned me, before I even knew which classroom I was in. From the moment I started my college career, I always felt out of place in the formal education space. I was constantly asked invasive questions about my personal life: when and how I planned to become a mother, if I had a partner, if I planned to get married. I spent hours in class listening to my professors dictate what, according to them, a "good woman" should do to be a "good professional" in higher education. However, in my third semester, the violence intensified when I decided to dedicate myself to social activism. My professors began to persecute me, conditioning my grades on my feminism and militancy. This semester, for the first time, a professor humiliated me in front of the entire class, saying that my success would always depend on how many people I was willing to please. I was 19 years old, the first time one of my professors decided to sexualize my professional capacity. This is a reality for women at all levels of education, at all levels of their professional career. I am 26 now and I know, I still don't live the last time this happens. As the years progressed, the violence not only persisted, but became more vicious. Professors made fun of the green scarf I wore tied to my suitcase, a symbol of my struggle, and jeered at me when I left class as I listened to them ridicule victims of sexual violence. In seventh semester, I was forced to read aloud a rape case in front of the class. I refused, and that decision cost me the semester. This constant series of abuses made me decide to speak out. I started with small peer groups, then seminars, and soon, I decided that I needed a formal and consistent space to support more people going through the same thing. When I turned 22, I decided to start a page on Instagram to collect anonymous testimonies of young women who were going through the same abuse in university classrooms and 4 years later, I lead the first organization in my country dedicated to accompany victims of educational violence to prevent them from dropping out of the higher education system. Today, my former professors continue to call me by names that are not mine and continue to question before the new generations the type of professional I have become. They continue to make up stories about my time in the classroom, trying to silence young women and keep them in fear. But now, surrounded by brave women, I feel the fear that once paralyzed me fading away, replaced by the certainty that safe spaces in universities are closer than ever to becoming a reality. Every day, my conviction in gender-sensitive education grows stronger, and I know that I will never regret risking my career to get this far. Today, I raise my voice with young women, so that no other has to survive higher education, so that we can all live our professional dreams, and so that the classroom is the path to our goals, not a cage that limits us. I remind myself everyday before I start working, that little Ljubi of 19 would´ve done anything to have a space like the one we are creating now to feel safe, I remind myself that feminist education can be the answer to gender inequality and I repeat to myself... Education must be feminist, or not be at all.

◆ ◆ ◆

STORY NUMBER 64

SAGE VOYAGEUR*
age: 24 years
Bujumbura, Burundi

As a woman, my journey with health and education has been both enriching and eye-opening. I've always been passionate about learning, but I've also had to face unique challenges related to my health. For example, I struggled with anxiety during my studies, which affected my concentration and performance. However, with proper support and mental health resources, I learned to manage my anxiety and excel academically. This experience not only strengthened me, but it also motivated me to advocate for the importance of mental health in women's educational journeys. I firmly believe that every woman deserves access to resources that support both her education and her health, so that she can realize her full potential. As a woman, my educational journey has been enriched by health challenges, particularly anxiety. With proper support, I learned to manage these challenges, which motivated me to advocate for the importance of mental health in women's education.

◆ ◆ ◆

ABOUT THE AUTHOR

Anya Sen

Anya Sen is a 16-year-old high schooler from New York City. She has been a girls' education and wellbeing activist, for over 9 years, working to fundraise and spread awareness about these causes. She has worked with multiple nonprofit organizations including Malala Fund, Foundation for Excellence, National Alliance on Mental Illness, and Turning Point for Women and Families. Anya also has her own nonprofit organization, Uplifting-Her, that provides advocacy for young women. You can follow more of Anya's work through her Instagram @anya_activism or the Uplifting-Her website (uplifting-her.org).

Printed in Great Britain
by Amazon